A PEN FITTER

SCRIBBLED NOTEBOOK

DIVYADHARSHINI R

To Lord Shiva without him, the Universe cannot function.

To Appa, you're my hero and my biggest inspiration ever. A man with the wholesome example of Hardwork. You're the one who can make me happy in every way. My heart and soul surround you every time.

To Amma, I can't step into the world without you. You make my place safer, protected me in every situation, and you are satisfied with my growth of lesser and higher. None can replace you in this world.

To Senthil Anna, You're my second father and protected me like a pearl in the shell. You are there with me when I need the home most. You're not expressive but I know you do care for me more.

To Deva (anna), I don't know what I'll do without you. My well-wisher, anytime available human, and the biggest asset in my life. Love which you have shown (unknown) reminds me that you still see me as a kid.

To My Angel, You made me strong, to face highs and lows, to satisfy me with your innocence, and to cheer with your smile when I am low. God's gift? No!!! God came as a gift.

Contents

Preface

A mixed emotion of a woman with tangled writings. The mixed theme of feelings and content expresses my biased mentality of me. Nature writer though, writing with scribbled emotions of love, hate, happiness, anxiety, and stress. I sincerely apologize, for the mistakes, I made in the book and hope you enjoy reading the tangled words, stanzas, and verses. Thank you for accepting my words on your list and have a good reading journey ahead.

1. Alive In Her Ripped Body

A tiny dot makes her happy,
She gave space to survive,
Stayed with blood and flesh of her,
Her intestines shrunken to help me grow,
Never worry about sharing her food,
Enjoyed each movement I made,
Ripped her body to make it alive.
A world seems to be scary
Embraced by her hug and smile,
Discerning her love wholly
When other ones are busy in life,
Wondering about unconditional love
One could shower wildly,
Greatest robustness in a lifetime.

2. First Adam

From being nothing to eat,
To become well known,
Your hard work which you hidden,
Not to show to your heir.
Loved your every sweat
Loved your every effort
Loved your every sacrifice
Loved you wholly
You're my world.
Still working for our benefits
We don't know how we'd repay you.
We consider you as the first Adam in the Universe.

3. An Island Dream...

Wide opened eyelids
Surrounded with greenery
Walked through wet leaves
Ways to somewhere.
Touched the droplets of tip
Fingers shivered and attracted veins
Roamed around what's next
Stood on a cliff and saw.
Flows like a storm never believed
Splashes through rock and sparkles
Sunlight shone brightly
Water twinkles like a mirror.
Beat up with a water
Body shrills and happiness bounds
Played like a kid never been
Physique got wet as well mental.
Turning around found none
Sported through lane
Found a big border sand
Thereby an ocean.
Running over water and fell
Feet were swinging with foam
Rummaging someone would alive
None present never mind.
Someone knocked on the door

Searching for it but nothing
Knock! Knock! Knock!
It's time to wake from a dream.

4. Proposal

You'd see the gorgeous blue carpet above
The day starts with a bright and warm
As such you.
Begin with smile
Make someone happy with your warmth
Dear girl, never worry about the past,
The present and future will be awesome
The path you take will be successful
Go, girl! The world is yours.
If you're agreed
Maybe the world of mine
Is you and only you!!
Waiting for a perfect opportunity
To explore the world with you
Hills, sea, sky, and Ice
Destinations are innumerable
Seated before you in a coffee house
At the view of Paris tower
Love city can adjust our love
It is waiting for your Yes!!
Say Yes!! My lady
We will get old together in 'the 80s.

5. My Beloved Diary

Started penning in grade five,
As the flow of ink knows,
The relationship between us,
Informing every low and high.
Day by day changes,
Proves life is a cycle,
A minute surprise jotted,
Worries are never forgotten.
When the right column indicates,
Months are passing by,
Had a clue that I have grown,
Letters kept prompt to explore.
Pages filled with emotions,
Happy, sad, angry, tear, sorrowful,
Apology, gratitude, love, and hatred,
Would be scripted and lasted longer.
Person met every day was unknown,
You know them well,
Reminds me of the future,
Laughed over their crossing in life.
A special one was written on a page,
Pouring all words to describe,
Enjoyed my craziness sometimes,
Keeping secret as a secret.
Turning you at sixty,

Smiling at some places,
Crying at some point,
Feeling just happened yesterday.
No human in the world,
Would come till the end of life,
Though immovable yet carries my eternal,
You're my best friend.

6. Kid at yard

Blossom of flowers drags,
Scented with nature's fragrance,
Beginning to the way of green,
A smile of the heart shows up,
Hearing the chirp of birds,
Flatters me to the wind,
Flying over the sky,
Reaching up to heaven,
The sound of a bee hustled,
Hustling back like a kid,
Running through the yard,
The rhythm of the beat,
Hears inside the body,
Chuckling when breeze touches,
Cheeks dance as wind chimes,
Longing for one more memory.

7. Mystic inferno

Furiously got into the mood
The thing which blasted out
A dragon resembles in face
Frightened till last and blocked.
Words are stagnant in the mind
Credited with maximum infuriating
Grudge has rolled oversoul
My body rammed like a hell.
Unlike other humans kept calm
Burst into tears as well
Convinced herself by weep
After half an hour rusting nerves wakes.
Got ready for the next schedule
Smiles with everything hidden
A woman like a mystic inferno
Heavenly angel well believed hell.

8. Pride Clicker

Looked aside turned around
Found none but eternal happiness
Lonely spread fingers on dried grass
Excited to move forward with her.
On the edge sat with cheeks
Hands gripped over the chin
She melts like a snow
On hearing of Koel.
Nothing was shown to the eye
The pleasant meal arrives
Food for her vision stood
Her hungry satisfied.
Waiting for the cubs to move
A giant body appears
Roars like a queen in the kingdom
Standing firm with pride.
Took her another eye from the backpack
Shot them with excitement
When she found another treat
Shocked with surprise and delight.
Steady walking King arrives
Various shots clicked
Happiness has no bound
Her dream was achieved and awarded.
Photographer for a reason

Yet watching Lion is her lifeline
Proudly said she is a woman
She can prove anything in the universe.

9. Waiting!!!

Tormented in way of living
Just came as lightening
For a second made brighter
Laughed, cuddled, in arms
Inseparable I think
Wrong judgment injured
Gone like a butterfly.
Meet me once
You'd know my value of missing
Missed, miss, missing you
Come back! My blood and veins
Are waiting to shower on you
The flesh is longing to cuddle
My heart is aching, come back soon.

10. Human being I inspired

Dawn to dusk a human works,
Looking out for all problems with ease,
Controlled by everyone but never worried,
Like a star shines every day with a smile.
Showering love for everyone without bias,
Wondering how much could tolerate,
Standing up like an iron rod,
Nothing could compare to strength.
If something happens to others,
Fights like a warrior and gets victory,
Couldn't bear the pain of a loved one's blood,
Dies by saving others.
Criticized by everyone which hurts,
Which you'd never reveal out,
The warmth you give makes comfortable,
No one in this world would be like you.
Got inspired by you,
As a woman, you brought up,
I will never make you low,
Mother!!! Bowing down to you for a lifetime.

11. Nature's Clown

Waking at the rays of light,
Making a day perfect,
Shining the brightest,
Yet, the world is the fullest.
Moving towards the window,
Sighting the tree's shadow,
Mere happiest picking
It lit up the face fuming.
Bestowing the errand of roses,
Figuring out the Earth's muses,
Clutching the feather,
A bird which sheds lower.
Stepping towards the yard,
Remembering life's hard,
Not in a goose down,
Hopping to the Nature's Clown.

12. "Mom"

C-section,
body ripped,
postpartum,
physique change,
tolerance,
challenges,
weeping for wept,
silent being and
best pain killer defines "Mom"

13. Daydream

Waves of thought,
Which comes back,
Started with one,
Ends with many.
When a teacher teaches,
The daydream starts,
Becoming an astronaut,
Flying to the moon.
There comes administrative,
Aspiring an IAS,
Drove with siren,
Flashes as lightning.
Here comes the teacher,
Dream who teaches,
Chalk and dust,
Gains respect among.
Finally, the daydream ends,
Bell rings for lunch,
Dreaming about a lunchbox,
Thinks about mom's stuffed.

14. Covid on Rich and Poor

Homelife which alienated,
Not much life of polluted,
Things become demanded,
Forgot not to be remembered.
Homelife which enjoyed,
Food and water possessed,
Movies that stalled,
Mattress knows weighed.
Life's not much easier,
People who roamed at the road,
Food and water-starved,
Child in hand and wept.
Not everyone's days are best,
Life is to be lived in peace,
Live your life with enough,
Think of people has none.

15. Nothing to Sky

Being nothing to seeing the sky,
Something cannot be changed,
Laying on the ground with an empty pocket,
Eyes filled with blue sky,
Teaches something that the world is small,
Moving forward doesn't work,
My heart sank to its stress,
Sky says "Wake up!!!,
You've more to do"
Woke and started walking to find
A new warm path brightens,
Found the real meaning of life.

16. Startled Reality

A subtle way of life,
Grilled in the middle of nowhere,
When the sky tears down apart,
Perhaps the Sun and Moon cried.
Squint in the eye,
The universe seems to be,
Like an endeavor,
The living beings hang.
Fault with social animals,
Nothing can be done with it.
Frenzy look made them exist,
Underrated fouls to be.

17. Waiting Veins...

My mind wanders,

My heart suffers,

Searching for you in life,

Which is the utmost priority,

Comeback to my world,

I will show you heaven,

Decorated with my flesh as flowers,

Veins as strings,

Blood as scent,

Do visit once you'll never give up,

Doors are opened,

Waiting for your arrival,

Come over and fill the space.

18. Stress

Stressed, Stress, Stresses, Stressing.
Never stops until I get swollen eyes,
Sore throat, heavy heart, and mentally ill.
Want to get rid of reality.
Need to dream and sleep forever.

19. Miss You

The days when we had giggles,
The days when we had excitements,
The days when we had Surprises,
The days when we had in arms,
The days when we had each other,
The day when we had our first argument,
The day when we had sour times,
The day when we get lost,
The "day" and "days" differ,
The timely problem comes,
And you went by.
Missed you and will not be missing you
You're not going to deal with my future,
Am going to stay happy as I wish,
No more dramatic but I'm sure I'll be happy without you

20. Unreal life

Unlike you, unless you,
United sometimes unique part,
Understand till underwent far,
Until I unknown real,
Unsigned wicked untied you,
Ungodly praised unsure future,
Unexpected ways unstable heart,
Unkind someone unintentionally happy.

21. Sleepless nights.

When I think of the past.
The sleep diminishes.
Hair that gets messy.
An ache in the head sustains.
My heart gets collapsed.
Wish I go back to the past.
Rewrite my whole story.

22. Waiting

Tormented in way of living
Just came as lightening
For a second made brighter
Laughed, cuddled, in arms
Inseparable I think
Wrong judgment injured
Gone like a butterfly.
Meet me once
You'd know my value of missing
Missed, miss, missing you
Come back! My blood and veins
Are waiting to shower on you
The flesh is longing to cuddle
My heart is aching, come back soon.

23. Zesty Zealous

Zeal in the process with zero-in-on,
Zigzag moving to reach zenith point,
Zapping as of zilch in treasure,
Zany to the world but zooming in,
Zinnober zooty always zingy,
Zion is made with zephyr and zither.

Thank you for reading till last. Hope you have enjoyed my tangled poems, stanzas, and words. I am grateful that you had chosen me and read my scribbled notebook. Thank you once again for your patience in reading and enjoying the lines.